POEMS OF PAIN

christina fatemi

Poems of Pain. Copyright 2024 by Christina Fatemi. All rights reserved. No part of this publication may be reproduced, distributed, or transmitted in any form or by any means, including photocopying, recording, or other electronic or mechanical methods, without the prior written permission of the publisher, except in the case of brief quotations embodied in critical reviews and certain other noncommercial uses permitted by copyright law.

For permission requests, write to the publisher, addressed "Attention: Permissions Coordinator," 205 N. Michigan Avenue, Suite #810, Chicago, IL 60601. 13th & Joan books may be purchased for educational, business or sales promotional use. For information, please email the Sales Department at sales@13thandjoan.com.

Printed in the U. S. A.

First Printing, July 2024.

Library of Congress Cataloging-in-Publication Data has been applied for.

ISBN: 978-1-7322479-2-5

Contents

Dedication	v	Wrong Choice	27
Poems of Pain	vi	Painful Colors	28
Introduction	1	Sinner's Prayer	29
LOVE	3	Tell Me	30
I BET	4	In the Heart	31
Struggling with Grace	5	Young	32
True Intentions	8	Love Hurts	33
Ocean	9	Dreams	34
With YOU	10	Hold On	35
Control	11	Falls Down	38
I Wrote this Poem for You	12	Fire	39
Naked	14	Feel Me	40
We Are	15	Missing You	41
Why?	16	Trying to Heal	42
Lies	17	Show Me	43
Hate Me	18	Forgive Me	44
Over It	19	Nut Case	45
Played Me	20	Demon	46
Life	21	Not Talking	47
Talk Again	22	Wake Up	48
Coexist	23	Aggressive	49
WHORE	24	Loving Me	50
Pressed	26	Ready	51
		Survival	52

Grandmothers House	53
3 AM	54
Checkmate	55
Child Support	56
Looking	57
CRAZY	58
Rico	59
Mental Block	60
Sade Song	61
COVID	62
Hard to Love	63
SHE WAS	64
I'm Her	65
Disconnected	66
Hype Sister Nadi	67
Stay Strong	68
Testimony	69
Purpose	70
Intention	72
Freedom	73
Conclusion	75
Author Bio	77

This book is dedicated to my son Rico. Thank you for opening my heart and saving my life. My love for you is unconditional. You humble me. The best journey I will ever endeavor is being your mother.

This book is also dedicated to my grandmother, Saundra Northington-Jackson, and my mother, Zina Fatemi. There aren't enough words that can express my love and appreciation...

Pain is defined as suffering or discomfort caused by illness or injury. It can also be an unpleasant or emotional experience. My life has been a collage of many forms of pain – physical, emotional, loss, heartbreak, abuse, and more. Pain seems to be naturally built into the human experience. Can we ever avoid or get around this feeling? That is the question.

Even when life seems to be great, there are still those moments of pain and sadness. We can go our whole lives trying to escape it, only for it to find us again. We must understand that pain is a part of our reality and journey. But there is no blueprint on how to deal with it when it knocks on our door. In many ways we are forced to be creative on how to allow pain to transform us in order to come out stronger. Pain teaches us and has a way of inspiring us to grow if we allow it.

You may ask, *Why* **Poems of Pain** if there is also love? I would counter with this question: *Have you ever loved someone so much that it hurt to the point you were broken?* There's that pain, again.

Poems of Pain is a body of work that expresses feelings derived from moments of sadness, days of confusion, and a deadly concoction of darkness, lust, sex, lows, love, loss, and loneliness. It takes you on a journey of vices turning into virtues. In times when my state of mind was immersed in an uncontrollable whirlwind of emotions mixed with depression, I was able to document the tumultuous path through my writings and poetry as a form of therapy. I carried these emotions from my past through the hardest years of my life. Through the darkness of those years, I found my light.

LOVE

What is this strange word? What is this feeling?

Is it real when people say it but don't mean it?
Is it real when people say it but don't show it?

I want to know it. Real love–not the superficial kind.
I want to experience a healing love that doesn't hurt.
I want to get lost in a strong love that doesn't fold.
I want to have a free love that allows me to express love–freely.
I don't want to be scared…

Scared to experience. Scared to get lost. Scared to have. Scared to be IN love.

Can somebody tell me: Where is my LOVE?

I BET

I bet you think this poem is about you,
maybe it is, maybe it isn't.

Struggling with Grace

Look at my face.
Do you see the strain? Not sure if I can mask my pain.
I think I'm insane with all that goes on in my brain.
I put on the front that makes you think that I'm ok. But I'm not ok.
Today may be a bad day.
I have no money,
A love that acts funny.
Do you see my pride when I step outside?
It should beam like armor. So no one can harm her.
Do you look into my eyes and wonder if I ever cry?
Lord, I would die if I couldn't have you inside.
It's a task to hide what you can't see.
It's hard and it hurts.
So, with my faith secured tightly in place,
I will continue to struggle with Grace.

grace

I have come to realize that struggles in life can eventually lead to something beautiful. They can help build character and make us stronger, more resilient individuals. I truly believe that it's all in how we deal with these struggles, with having faith in God, keeping purpose in mind and our willingness to push through with the hope of a positive outcome.

My first experience with emotional pain happened when I was just 5 years old, when my parents divorced. That was followed by sexual abuse and toxic abusive relationships. I internalized all of this pain, not knowing how to connect with my own emotions. It wasn't until I became a single mother at the age of 22 that I truly began to understand what it meant to struggle.

I lived in survival mode, constantly worrying that I would lose myself. After giving birth to my son I had become financially dependent on my son's father and didn't focus on my personal career goals. Then when he lost his career, the child support I was accustomed to stopped. I struggled to find work and had to move in with my grandmother. On top of everything else, I was diagnosed with celiac disease and endometriosis, which added chronic physical pain to the mix.

Despite all of these struggles, I never let them show to others. I always put my son's needs first and tried never to let anyone see me in a negative light. I lived by any means necessary, even if it meant making decisions I wasn't proud of. It wasn't until I started to focus on my healing and let go of living in survival mode that I began to see a change. I found my faith in God and self-love, forgave myself and others who had hurt me, and made self-care a priority.

As I went through my healing process, some relationships changed for the better, while others fell away. I set boundaries and defended myself, which didn't sit well with everyone. But I knew I couldn't go back to the hurt and survival mode of my past. I was a new person, and I was never going to allow anyone or anything to take me back to that dark place.

True Intentions

I could write until my fingers bleed about how real this feeling was for me. I could tell you exactly how I feel, but I don't want to take the chance, not knowing if you will care. I must question if our connection was even real. Expressing emotion can be a bitch and while I want to tell you, I have a feeling that words will probably fail me.

Was my wanting you too much for you? Was it something I said that pushed you away? I was ready for forever, but you showed me that the feeling was temporary. Couldn't you see my heart? Couldn't you read my thoughts? I wanted what I know I couldn't express. I could show you my feelings if I wasn't so pressed – pressed not to be hurt. I could tell you that I'm different, but are you going to believe me? Can you see how real I am or is that hard to see? Am I what you want?

I don't want to talk to you physically. I just want to hear your soul. I want to communicate with the person that not many know. Not the ego or the hurt, just the one I met first. Even though you're hood, shit STILL could be good. But ONE thing made you flip. Then, you dipped. My intentions were true. What about you?

Ocean

Something about your energy has me open, I'm connected to your soul as the depths of you flow in. Like waves, I want to roll, I want to take control.

We could be as one in the sand, making love in different lands.
There is no limit to this emotion. My love goes deep like the ocean.

My vision peers beyond your pain; And your words keep swimming around in my brain. One touch from you and I know I'll go insane....

I'm ready for whatever even if it's all in my head,
This could be forever if we just keep sailing ahead.

Ocean love.

With YOU

Even when we are apart, we're connected
Unbothered and unaffected.
Boy, I swear you got my heart.
And if we are taking one day at a time, I can handle that part.
In due time, together we'll shine
As I heal your wounds, you'll heal mine.
I can't wait for you to put a baby in my womb,
New life, new dreams, for us are coming soon.
I don't care what they say – I'll be with you anyway.
When I'm with you, I'm in the zone
Loved and protected, never alone.
Being with you is home.
I can't wait for the day, the hour, the minute, the second that I am with you again.

Control

You act as if you really care,
But the truth is you were never there.
No commitment or expectations
But as soon as I became free
You come running back to me.
There's no room left here to twist and turn me around.
I made a vow, this time, I won't let myself down.
If you ever needed anything, I was the one there.
But after what you've done, why should I care?
You want to torture me and play with my emotions.
Knowing my heart for you is so much more than a notion.
So now I'm numb. All I feel is cold.
I wanted love. All you wanted was control.

I Wrote this Poem for You

I miss you in bed.
I'm missing us and want to get back to the good space we had.
I don't like this distance and the tension is killing me.
I just want to kiss and hold you.
Don't you know that I adore you?
I want you to come over.
Let me make love to you with all of my passion.
I want it wild and crazy, so I can see your reaction.
Give me each stroke with power, don't you dare stop
And once you finish, I'll taste every single drop.
I don't want to break up.
I just want to make up.
I'll do anything for you.
We were meant to be.
If only you could see…

Naked

The glance I stole out of the window reminded me of how beautiful the rain is. I am in constant awe of the sound. His body next to mine, naked. We talk about life. We openly share our truths. There are no lies between us. He touches me intimately with no reservation. Raw pleasure is our choice. And with every kiss, our bodies grow warmer and closer. I hold on tighter and stronger just as his excitement leads to our collective climax. We stare into one another's eyes. One sees into the other's world. Just like that, we are completely lost in each other. This might be love. I want to see where this goes. I'll take that journey with you, wearing nothing at all. Naked.

We Are

Man, we have so much more work to do. My job holds such a heavy energy.

Women suffering everywhere—all from different backgrounds with different stories; all bearing the same pain.

I ask myself: Am I one of them?

I must be. We are never too far from one another. We simply have different life experiences sharing the same reality: We are human.

Why?

Why should you just get away with it?
It's not fair.
I need you to own up to it.
I stand alone in the dark, unable to clear my head.
Recognizing that what's understood doesn't need to be said.
My heart hurts. I feel lost.
I once had you. Now, you're gone.
Fuck it–we can't ever do this again.

Lies

Keep it on the down low? HELL NO!
I'm not keeping quiet just because you don't want that bitch to know.
If you're going to be with me, I'm going to be the only one.
I'm not about those games, boy.
You can walk the other way, boy.
Now I know what you said were just words.
NO action, NO intent, just stuff I already heard.
And words can't hold me, kiss me, or tell me everything is going to be alright.
Your words are empty lies that have no meaning.

Hate Me

I don't know why you hate me.
Who would ever want to live like this?
I try not to let it get to me
But when I think about what you did to me,
I don't know why you hate me.

I don't know why you hate me.
Is my only allowance to watch you walk away?
All the signs and signals said you weren't the one
But I ignored the red flags, each and every one.
I don't know why you hate me.

I don't know why you hate me.
What did I ever do to you but love you?
You definitely had a way of making me feel
Like I deserved to be treated like a trick.
In return, I looked like the crazy chick.
Whatever cocktail we were, it damn sure didn't mix.
We could never get things right; our best stance was a fight.
Every month, every week–just violence, no peace. I tried everything.
And still, I don't know why you hate me.
But maybe, just maybe, I hate myself…

Over It

It's not permanent; I can get over it. You make it so easy to just get over it. You have nothing to share, so why should I care? I'm cursed with you. I'm always sad and blue. I might not see my way through, but I can see right through you. You're the only one who can't love me, and one day you're going to miss me. You'll never ever see me, 'cause I'm really about to do me. Can't believe I was so free for someone who didn't even take the time to know me. Is this reality?

Everyone said from the start that you were going to break my heart. I'll give it to you-you played me, but this pussy is still amazing! So, I'll bounce back and give it another try. I'll never let another tell me this many lies. All your pictures have been burned; every hard lesson learned. And I'll never give respect in a place where I know that shit wasn't earned.

My mind no longer races, my feet no longer pace. I think about it constantly just so I'll never go back to that place where you hurt me. I can't help but wonder how things would be if the spell you had me under had broken. Life still goes on and I don't want to be alone, but the way you act dictates that I have to move on. No more drama. No more control. How does a guy like you stay breathing without having a soul? All you do is this. Caught up in the sex, but not in person–making the stabbing pain I feel worsen. You never loved me, there's no colder shit than this. You went in too deep. Now, I'm over it.

Played Me

Don't think I ever felt loved, but I loved you.
Heard the words, but the actions were untrue.
Said you cared with the same mouth that cursed me
Said I was nothing all while you hurt me.
Am I nothing or am I crazy?
I'm still human, you should have saved me.
Somehow, I thought I'd forever be your lady…

I know I get a little edgy, but baby he made me crazy.
I don't think you even understand how he played me.
Understand this: I need YOU to save me!

Give me some medicine
All I want is to be well again.
Don't question me about what I should have done.
Trust me, I'm moving on from him.
I don't want to be needy, but baby I am
I need you to help me forget about him.

Life

I have been thinking a lot about life lately.

I guess this is what happens when you hit a certain age and you're like "Oh Shit! We really only get ONE life?"

And what am I going to do with the rest of mine to ensure that I will be happy?

Sometimes, my thoughts wander….

What if I didn't make that mistake?
What if I went down another path?
What would my life be like?
Do you ever wonder sometimes?

I guess every day is a chance God gives us to make us believe. It's a chance to make ourselves better. It's a chance to be happy, even on our worst days. A bad day is bad, but it is still a day lived and an experience learned.

So many things happen to so many people. No one walks the same walk as another. So how do you know where they have been or where they're going?

The questions we must ask in this life…

Talk Again

They're just words, baby.

I'm angry. I don't mean it.

All I asked you to do was be loyal, but you didn't.
All you really did was put me through it.
I'll survive trying to let it go and get through it.

It's calm right now but the storm is coming, and it's going to rain so hard.

I can feel it in my heart.

But when the storm passes, there will be light. And a rainbow.

Maybe then……. we can talk again.

Coexist

Why can't we coexist?

God created us for this one world but clearly, I'm not your one girl!

Even still, we need to try to coexist to stay alive.

You fight to kill, and I have a strong will. To live?
I want to love. I want to give my all.
I want to give my heart, but you block it with a wall.
It's a crushing downfall for us to exist
Because in this life we can't coexist.

Why can't we coexist?

WHORE

I feel like when I'm here I always think...I think about what I want. And if what I want involves you. Maybe it doesn't. What I know is that I don't want to lose you, so I chose you. I chose you to hurt me. I chose you to let me down because that's all you do. You force me to walk away when all I want to do is cry and stay. Do you care about how I feel? Do you care about what's real? I drive myself crazy not knowing. I can't help but think about you and the things you do. How you fucked me out of control–then rolled. You know what you did to me! How can I have dignity when you take that away from me? When I call you, you always ignore. So, tell me the truth-am I just your whore?

anger

Pressed

I told myself I wouldn't bother.
I wouldn't call. But what did I do? I called. I bothered. Shit.

What the fuck are you doing? I haven't heard from you all day. Now, my head is spinning.

I don't know what I'd do if you were right here right now.
But I wish you were right here right now.

Nothing I say can keep these feelings away.
Never really talked about my place in your life. But I hope I have one.
I don't know if I'm coming or going–but I know it's all because of you.

I didn't ask for you. In fact, you came for me.

I don't know what I'm going to do but shit, seems like it could be so right with you.

Is it too early to say I love you?

Wrong Choice

I had a choice not to feel this way.
I promised myself I wouldn't do it!
That I couldn't do it anymore, but what did I do?
I went and did it.
Same outcome, different story.
How many times do I have to feel this pain?
I am starting to think I'm the one that's insane.
Am I addicted to pain?
How can I blame you when I kept coming back to you?
I'm ashamed.
Why did you want to hurt me so bad?
Why did I even love you?
There's nothing I want from you.
It's crazy because I hate what you did to me.
I just feel so empty.
Each day the Lord fills me, so how can I feel so sad inside?
I made the wrong choice and wasted my time.
Still, somehow I end up on your line.

Painful Colors

I never want to feel this again.
I never want to feel this pain again.

Leave me alone.
I want to get away from all this.

Beautiful flowers surround me, making up all different colors around me.
I can almost see the sunshine. I need it.

The colors heal me. The colors shield me. But they hurt.

I never want to feel this again.

Sinner's Prayer

God,

Please take my karma and let bygones be bygones. I repent of all my sins and ask you to make me whole!

Thank you for blessing and keeping me, in spite of me and my shortcomings. I am asking you to continue looking over us each day and grant us your favor in righteousness.

Please forgive me! I want to walk without shame knowing that even a sinner can be born again. Don't crucify me and my name. Protect me from my enemies. Cleanse me again and extend me your most precious guidance and mercy that I may fear no evil.

Please place your loving hands of protection and promise over my son, Rico. I beg of you–please don't make him pay for my misfortune. My sins are my cross to bear. Help me fulfill my purpose and ultimately give me the desires of my heart.

I pray you accept this sinner's prayer.

Amen

Tell Me

You are like so many who have come to me...
What are you going to do with me?

In the Heart

In the heart, you can find many things: love, joy, hurt, pain, and rejection. All of these feelings can move you in different directions. Why do we use the phrase, "with all my heart?" Do we really love with our hearts or do we love with our heads? Are the two actually separate?

My heart won't let me go, but my mind is telling me no. I have to wonder if a broken heart ever really heals. Help me understand!

When it comes to love, I feel so alone in this world. The heart beats and we know it. But when the heart breaks, we feel it. And we know the sound of a broken heart. So now, I'm searching for what will heal my heart. I've lost my desire for love. I don't even want to know what it feels like anymore.

If I put my heart in your hand, will you take it? Will you hold it with care? Or will you do what everybody else did–break it? Tell me what you're going to do. I need to know.

Young

Why is it that I have to be so strong in such a weak world? It's cold. I want so badly to fulfill my destiny. I want it with everything in me. My life is nowhere near complete. There's so much I want to see.

When I was five, I dreamed of starring in a movie. I always imagined I would play the role of a princess or someone who was super glamorous. After all, in my mind, I WAS a princess. My game of "make-believe" made me a foreign beauty from a faraway land in a fairy tale. That was not my story.

In reality, my mother married my father at nineteen, had me at twenty-two, and divorced him at twenty-eight–for another woman. I don't know if my mother living in her truth was a gift or a curse. Now that I'm an adult, I've learned how to appreciate my mother for not exposing me to another man. At the same time, I was never able to see the way a man SHOULD treat a woman. All I knew was my parents weren't together and I didn't like how that felt.

I vowed that when I grew up and had a baby, I would never leave my child's father. Wishful thinking of a heart and mind, so young.

Love Hurts

If it wasn't love, it wouldn't hurt.
You have to love someone to be able to hurt them.
I hurt you, you hurt me–what are we going to do?
It goes so far that love turns to hate.
Then the feelings we had get completely erased.
The pain runs so deep.
I still weep.
We don't have to pretend.
We can at least be friends.
It's true what they say–love hurts.

Dreams

Photographic dreams of a new reality.
Checking for my future, I no longer see my past.

If you truly loved me, why didn't you make it last?

Fake is the new real.
Superficial will get you places you want to go.

Hell, I don't know. How can you be so cold, not to think about responsibility?

Love and care about me now, but leave me desperately.

Hold On

You don't want me but you find a way to hold on.

Control is what you want.

You can't even see it, but everyone wants me to move how they move.
I'm moving two different ways, being pulled in opposite directions.
It's ripping us apart.

Why can't you just think like me?
Why are we so much alike, yet so different?

I try not to get caught up in your negativity but it overtakes me.
You're an empty black hole–things go in and never seem to return.

But you always return.

I can't get you out of my mind, even as time passes by.
I'm lost in sadness without you. And with you.

Life can be a confusing journey, filled with moments that overwhelm and isolate us. It's easy to feel lost in a world that is both beautiful and terrifying, but holding on to people, places, and things that don't bring us value is ultimately futile. Others may only see our wounds and use them to inflict even more pain, but we have the power to avoid such suffering.

When we finally open our eyes and refuse to conform to the facades of the world around us, we experience a transformation that clears away the dust and debris of our lives. Achieving this clarity requires pulling God close and becoming more self-aware in the process. Only then can we fully understand the world and our place within it. Let's embrace our vulnerability, push past the pain, and discover the truth that lies within.

Faith is a key component to our relationship with God. Trusting in the greater good that will align for us even through periods of pain and difficulties.

Falls Down

It eventually all falls down. Looking back, it took me longer to achieve than to lose. My story is far from a fairytale. I guess you could say I have been a little naive. Life can bring so much but can take so much away. Even in a brand-new Range Rover, I was struggling. Where did it start?

I don't want to love anymore. Every time I do, I get hurt.

I don't want to give anymore. Everyone I give to just takes from me.

I don't want to trust anymore. Everyone I trust lies.

No more, no more, NO MORE!

If you loved me, you would have stayed. I'm tired of the games. Be who you say you are! I guess it's true what they say–nothing stays the same. Things change, but you always do the same old thing. You want to destroy me. You want to move me. You want to force me to believe you, but the only thing I want to do is leave you.

Fire

Release this fire inside of me!

I'm going insane with what's in my brain.

Baby daddy drama and lack of income.

But something is telling me, my time is coming!

Feel Me

The heart carries so much anguish,
Why must we live this way?
Everything you have ever done
Can somehow be overcome.
I was a perfectly wrapped present.
Now, I'm undone.

I'm living life like you and hurting like you,
But reality reminds me I'm nothing like you.
My mind is eternally hopeful. One day, love will find me.

Don't empty my soul. I want to be ready for you should you find hope and faith.

Unfortunately, I lost you in the ocean of lies.
And now, all I can do is cry.
Can you hear me when I call you?
Can you feel my broken heart?
I love you and I hate you at the same time.
In everything I do, I'm broken and halfhearted.
And now it's hopeless: We are dearly departed...

Missing You

I miss you. I can't be with anybody because of the way you did my body.
You got me thinking all crazy. When I'm just trying to be with you, baby.
You take my mind to different places.
Don't know what it is about you that I'm craving.
Maybe it's your touch. I think it's your kiss.
Memories of you in my past thinking why it didn't last.
This time though, I'm never letting go.
Let me know what I got to do, to get back next to you...
I'll do it how you want. With me, it's never been a front.
We can get so deep and real. It's only you that I feel.
So loyal, it would make you spoiled.
And I can't shake the feeling I get when I'm with you.
Our conversations fuck my mind. Every time we talk, I lose track of time.
This connection is rare; long strokes and deep stares.
Please baby let me know what I got to do to get back next to you...

Trying to Heal

Under the stars of the universe, I cry.
With an open heart and no pride, I just want to try.
Give me wings so I can fly.
Turning points in life can't be taught, you have to go with your gut.
My feelings are real; positive thoughts of knowing and wanting to grow.
Outside of this loneliness being taken for granted. I truly can't take it.
Sometimes I don't know if I'll make it.
You took advantage of me and I can't fake it.

Show Me

Show me that real love,
Because I never knew it.
He asked me, "Do you even know how to love a man?"
Back then I didn't even understand.

Forgive Me

Forgive me for not loving myself enough to love you.
Forgive me for my pain.
Forgive me for trying to heal.
Forgive me for being selfish.
Forgive me for my negative thoughts.
Forgive me for not changing fast enough.
Forgive me for not understanding.
Forgive me for my words.
Forgive me for my bad moves.
Forgive me for needing you like I do.
Please forgive me…

Nut Case

In a rage, I spin.
I can't even see.
I don't know if this is even me.
I'm calling your phone
Can't leave you alone.
You don't want to be with me,
But I'm not letting you go.
Then, I lose control.
It's like this every time.
I want you to be mine.
If I can't have you then…
Die!

Demon

This demon is trying to steal my happiness.
This demon wants me to believe everyone is against me.
This demon won't let me heal.
This demon is trying to take me.
This demon is trying to break me.

There is a demon inside of me
It needs to leave. I need to be delivered
I ask God for help because I can't do it myself.

Not Talking

Where did the love go? Why aren't we talking?
You were just here in my bed!

It's been too long for you to not call. Do you not want me at all?
Is it really over? No! Can we start over?

You meant something to me. Baby, please call me.

Wake Up

I can't sleep.
Nothing brings me peace.
I wish I could wake up from this dream.
I wish he wasn't so mean.
In the depths of my soul, I lost control.
I never knew how bad it was.
I want this energy to be clear.
I want to understand why I'm here.
So many times, I've lost when I thought I was winning.
I was so happy but didn't know what to do.
The space you held in my bed is cold.
My insides are empty.
Everything feels different.
I don't want to be here without you.
I want to hold you and love you.
I called you all night and you didn't answer.
I just wanted to talk to you.
I wanted to make it right with you, but it only pushed you further away.
I know it's over; I know we can't be.
I had dreams of us, a house, and a kid.
I was going to give my all. All I could give.
I now know it was you all along.

Aggressive

You pull me close. Too close.

I tell you no, but you're not trying to hear me.

I told you where I am.

I don't want any distractions with this love, but you are pushing me.
Harder and harder.

Trying to move in quick, but I don't want the dick. Leave me alone. It's time to go home.

Loving Me

Loving me isn't easy.
I know you do in many ways.
You loved me when I wasn't my best.
You spoke to my spirit.
Every inch of you lives inside me.
There is nothing I can hide.
There is no pride.
You love me more than I love myself.
I need help.

Ready

As I go into the next chapter, a few things are clear.

The lost little girl with trauma she couldn't fathom is ready to move forward.

She will be ok.

She is healed of her past.

And now she understands–it all happened for a reason. That reason was necessary for this season.

It has been an amazing year for her because she believed in herself.

She taught me–I'm worth everything.

Survival

I'm moving out of this way of life. From surviving to living.
I was just getting by.
I just wanted to be free—from the pain, from things that tried to control me, from the things that were sent to destroy me.
Living freely with ease, I smile at the thought. Could it even be possible to live like this and not be restricted by circumstance? In my mind, there's a glance. Survival is hard and the truth is, I'm way too scared.

Grandmothers House

Driving back and forth to a low paying job, barely making it to next week. Gotta fuck a nigga just to eat. But one day I'll be ok. I'll be in my own house anyway. I'll be driving in my Benz, call it what you want. I'm just trying to be set up. Taking care of my son while collecting my funds. Dreaming of better days while I'm here. Outside in an old Toyota smoking a joint. Probably going to catch this flight on saturday to get laid and a bill paid. Ready to move out. I'm just trying to be set up.

3 AM

I texted you "I love you," and you didn't reply. Went to sleep with tears in my eyes. Woke up and you replied, "I love you too."

I almost died.

Checkmate

I thought you knew better than to think I wasn't going to find out. Looking past the shit you say cause most of it is fake anyway. You're a preacher in fake clothes. It's a shame nobody knows. The words you speak aren't even in the depths of your soul. The devil got you on a high road..

Child Support

I thought I understood, but now I'm confused.
I look down at your feet to see a fresh pair of designer shoes.
This mentality is so backward and it's making me sick.
No car, house, or job–but brand-new kicks?
Somehow, you can buy those but conveniently disagree
To pay what you know is your legal responsibility. Always with different women having babies.
Every time I think about this it brings me down.
So much, I almost want to turn the money down.
I have to bear the weight while you do whatever you want living so free.
And now I have to be a superwoman, for my kid, and for me.

Looking

Looking for a man of God who has a job, stands 10 toes down and loyal when I'm not around. A man who is secure with himself and not trying to be like anyone else. A man who cares and is always there. Strong and shows emotion. Leads with compassion. Positive when things get tight, knows how to fight. Passionate about his morals and values. A king whose energy shins bright. Respected in his community. Not afraid to speak the truth, lives in his truth and purpose. Divine Masculinity. Loves and mentors the youth. Treats me like a Queen, protects and provides. A man I don't have to hide. A man who loves me for me. I never have to ask or beg. Studies my mind, body and soul. Feeds my spirituality along with his. Takes us to new levels. We pray together. Our bodies connect so intensely that making love turns to art. Seeing each other fully with understanding. We are each other's peace and home. I'm really not looking but God will find prayfully all in due time.

CRAZY

They wanted to count me out, labeled me all kinds of crazy; all because I caught on to how they were trying to play me. They smiled in my face while I was suffering just so they could feel better about themselves, jealous the whole time of my eternal shine. Once I started to heal, everything was revealed–the hate and the lies all of them tried to hide. No one was really by my side. I was simply a benefit for them when it was convenient. They talked about me behind my back all while wanting to be like me. I thought they were my friends. It hurt like hell to find out it was all fake. All they did was take. They even downplayed me as a woman with no emotion; no respect for me but acting like they were perfect. They tried to tell my story because they don't know their own. They attempted to gaslight me into a frenzy…

But am I crazy?

Or is it the other way around? I see evil. You victimize yourself out of accountability. If I am crazy, I'll embrace this crazy.

Cause y'all bitches are shady.

Rico

I love being your mother.
I gave up my wrongs for your right.
I am the vessel that God used to birth you.
In giving it to you, you saved my life.
How blessed am I that He gave you to me?
You take the pain away with your smile and personality.
Your hugs are heaven, warm works of art.
My only baby boy, my joy, my heart…

Mental Block

Took me months to see through the pain.
Mentally, I think I was going crazy.
On the outside, I seemed fine.
On the inside I was sad, numbing the pain in my world.
I wasn't sure of my path or where I was going.
It seemed like everyone had it figured out when I was just living in confusion.
What was stopping me from figuring out my life? So many questions in my mind.
All I wanted was a break–a pause from the drama or anything negative.
I need to be at peace within myself.
I need to stop the war of life that is a constant fight.
I no longer want to waste my time on people, places, and things that aren't worth my energy.
I have to unblock the mental block.

Sade Song

It was the Sweetest Taboo the way he had me.
IS IT A CRIME to go this hard?
A Smooth Operator he is.
This is no Ordinary love.
At times I feel like I don't deserve it, but I hang on to your love.
I only wanted to be By Your Side because your Love is KING.
It's like Paradise to be in your arms.
You give me the Kiss of life and it makes me think nothing can come between us.
I cherish the DAYS we spend.
You are the moon and the sky.
I will never leave you because Love is stronger than Pride.

COVID

You think you got me, but my mind is stronger.
You are fucking with a fighter, one who truly goes harder.
Can't believe you caught me slippin but never again.
I got a life to live and you're not going to be my end.
My son needs me so you can't have me.
I never want this feeling again.
Get out of my body and out of my mind.
This is my moment. This is my time.
I'm reclaiming my life. It's dedicated to God.
I have a purpose; I'll reach it and beyond.
I didn't make it this far and go through everything I have to stop here.
I have to beat this; I will beat this. I have beat this COVID.

Hard to Love

WHY AM I so hard to love?
When love is all I give to you.
You have no clue, the way you talk to me turns me blue.
I'm depressed with all this emotion but can't even let you know it.
You say I'm hard to love but all I want is a hug.

SHE WAS

Before she was… Before she was… Before she was… Lost.

I'm Her

I've been hot, I've been that. And nothing is stopping me now.

I'm passing my own past. You won't even understand my ways until you come over to this side. I can't take everyone with me. God's confidence, not mine. The people who second-guessed me are about to miss me. I'll never trade my soul to the world so cold but it's hot in hell?, I can't tell. Either way, I'm going to be OK and my son is rich. I've been that BITCH…

Disconnected

Disconnected from this space.
Disconnected from my body. My head is in another place.
Not feeling like myself, every day it's something.
Making something out of nothing.
Dreaming, floating away. Yet, still I stay.
I cry tears of joy in the morning. Thanking God for each moment.
The highs and the lows but still I roll…
Do you feel me?

Hype Sister Nadi

It's going to be hard to not hear from you. Who's gonna hype me like you do? You know, the way you would always come through – GIRL, I LOVED YOU!

Thank you for always being true.

That outgoing personality and energy. Like a star, you shined so bright.

My hype sis: You surely will be missed. I know now, with God, you are resting in peace.

Stay Strong

My body hurts every day finding ways to push through. Is the mind stronger than the body? Can I fake like I don't feel it? If I even talk about it, will anyone even want to hear it? Doctors don't really help when you need healing. I need healing and can't take medicine for this feeling. I know it will never go away but through all the pain, I stay.

Testimony

You know God is working but you may not understand where He has you. God has shown me so much grace. I can remember the times I've been down. Then, out of nowhere, He raises me up–those were miracles. Faith in God was my only source of strength through pain. God healed me. I thank God for His continued healing and deliverance in my life. For Him to see fit to keep me on this earth for a little longer each day I raise means so much. To be able to be a mother. It was His concrete proof to me that He STILL has purpose and plans for my life. Now, I know what it means when they say He sees the best in you. God is good! So many times, I let the world, family, friends, and haters name me. But now I have let God name me. Thank you, God, for renaming me: Blessed, Redeemed, Forgiven, Victorious, Overcomer, Loved, Queen Mother, and Masterpiece.

Purpose

Purpose requires pain–same way the earth needs the rain.

healing

Intention

With this life I am conflicted, with all things abusing my mind and time. Energy wasted on not connecting with the most high, getting high drinking the dark life. How much do we love it? growing through it. Reaching higher hurts more but I gotta give that life up, In his name I trust. I know I am chosen. Set apart in his likeness. So now I walk away and pray. I don't need the sex, alcohol and material things to make me feel alive. I am here with no pride, I let go of the ego's need to have more. Thanking the most high for another day to get it right. I will be wrong many times and repent but I know to whom I represent.

Freedom

Freedom from my own destruction
Freedom from fear
Freedom from stagnation
Freedom from depression
Freedom from loneliness
Freedom from the darkness in my mind
Freedom from the fake
Freedom from stress
Freedom from anger
Freedom from survival
Freedom to be real
Freedom to love
Freedom to trust
Freedom to hold space
Freedom to be present
Freedom to speak my mind
Freedom to grow
Freedom to be at peace
Freedom to give
Freedom to live
Freedom to just be…Free

Conclusion

We tend to believe pain is a punishment, but really it's just a process. By being hurt, it inevitably leads us to healing. What I have learned is that when we let go, our true power evolves. Holding onto feelings, past emotions, trauma, and anger will only hold us back even further. Experiencing pain doesn't have to dictate your life. We will not be able to reach our true potential carrying the past. Letting go invites healing. Letting go puts your mind at ease. You're no longer giving your power away. You stop worrying about what someone has done to you or why something didn't go your way. Moving forward with ease allows you to be more aware, present, and positive. When you truly focus on how to make YOU a better person, you have reached the bridge to your highest potential. Easier said than done, right? It's not an overnight process, and I'm still processing. Healing can take many years and then something else arrives that may require you to start the process over. It's okay! Some situations are out of our control, and it's ultimately God's Will. You can't rush the process. Allow yourself to feel, forgive, and love yourself over again. Pain is a natural phenomenon but suffering is a choice, and I choose not to suffer.

Author Bio

Christina Fatemi, a Baltimore, MD native, discovered her passion for writing and journaling during her teenage years.

As a first-time author, Christina's work is a testament to her raw expression of feminine emotions and candid experiences of love, healing, and pain. Her writing delves deep into personal struggles and her journey of connecting to spirituality, blending elements to create an authentic and captivating reading experience for her audience.

Beyond her writing endeavors, Christina is a devoted single mother who understands the challenges faced by other single mothers. Christina strives to encourage and support single motherhood, displaying her compassion and dedication to positively impacting the lives of others within her community.

In her journey as both a writer and a mother, Christina's story is one of resilience. Her work stands as a powerful testament to the process of transformation, freedom from past selves, and the power of faith to overcome.

www.ingramcontent.com/pod-product-compliance
Lightning Source LLC
Chambersburg PA
CBHW042359070526
44585CB00029B/2992